Trapped In
Earthquake Canyon

Personal Account of Surviving the 1959 Hebgen Lake Earthquake

Cynthia Roberts Brunnette

Willard Dean Roberts

Douglas Brunnette, editor

Published by Nature's Mountain Press LLC

naturesmountain@msn.com

Library of Congress Control Number: 2017919582

ISBN: 0999732803

ISBN-13: 978-0999732809

Dedication

In memory of those who lost their lives and to those
who survived the 1959 Hebgen Lake Earthquake

Contents

Acknowledgments

Gratitude is extended to:

Douglas Brunnette for editing

Brenden Brunnette for his work on the photos and cover of the book

Gloria Roberts and Nancy Roberts for sharing their memories and photos

John Owen for providing the front cover photo

Preface

In college, while taking a sociology class, my professor told us that we would never be remembered unless we had posterity or wrote a book. I followed part of his advice and had four children but never got around to writing a book. For many years, I have been encouraged by my husband and children to record my memories of a cataclysmic event my family experienced when I was a child. Then something unexpected happened! As I was going through some items in my closet, I found my father's own written words about our experience. His style of descriptive writing painted a unique literary picture of that fateful night and following day. I believed that his story was too good to be buried somewhere on a shelf. I wanted to share his words with posterity and with anyone interested in this natural disaster.

My father, Willard Dean Roberts, wrote his account of the disaster in December of 1959. He passed away in July of 2009. I decided to intertwine my memories with his. My mother, Gloria Roberts, is still living and her recollections are included as well as those of my sister, Nancy Roberts.

Dad never knew that he would write a book with me! It is like Natalie Cole singing a duet with her father, Nat King Cole, years after his death. It has been fifty-eight years since that night of terror. I can vividly recall what happened. We were there! My family survived the August 17th, 1959, Hebgen Lake Earthquake.

Chapter One

A Family Vacation Begins

What follows is an account of events of the 1959 Hebgen Lake Earthquake written by my father W. Dean Roberts and myself, Cynthia Roberts Brunnette. Dean's actual unedited words from 1959 are combined with my personal recollection of what our family experienced during this horrific natural disaster.

Cynthia: It was the summer of 1959 when my parents decided to take a family vacation. The workers for Kennecott Copper, where my father was employed, were out on strike. This seemed to happen frequently in those days. It was August and it did not look like the strike was going to end any time soon. Being out of work was stressful and my parents needed a break. I was an only child when we took our last vacation, and now I had a sister. We were all nature lovers so we desired to go somewhere beautiful, serene, and peaceful. A decision was made to go to the Yellowstone

National Park area. That way, Dad could get some fishing in and we could observe wild life. The thought of fishing was not too exciting to me. I was constantly getting my line tangled or snagged and I reeled in more junk than I did fish.

Dad: The sign read "West Yellowstone, Montana." It was looming at me dead ahead. I had been anxious to see this sign, and as I looked across the hood of my new car, its yellow-painted metal glinting softly in the afternoon sun, I warmed at the thought of this vacation — the first for my family in five years. The date was August 17, 1959. I had left Salt Lake City accompanied by my wife and my two daughters at 3:30 a.m. Our plans were varied in intent for coming to Yellowstone National Park. I wanted to do some fishing. My wife Gloria, because of the advice of her doctor, wanted to rest and relax. My eight year-old, Cynthia, just wanted a vacation away from home. For her first vacation, three year-old Nancy wanted to see the bears — oh, how she wanted to see real bears! We had planned to stay in West Yellowstone the first night and then go into the Park the following day. A feeling floated through me in a fluid-like motion — it was happiness. I could sense it in my family, too. Mounting problems had been engulfing us back home, so for a few days we were leaving them behind.

Cynthia: We packed up our new yellow Mercury sedan early in the morning of Monday, August 17, 1959, and headed from our home near Salt Lake City, Utah, to our destination in Montana. My sister, Nancy, remembers that she was allowed to bring one toy. She decided to take a small stuffed bear. According to my mother, we stopped in Idaho Falls for some pancakes. That was a traditional thing for our family to do.

Dad: The tires skimmed the remaining highway into town and whispered musically as we pulled in and slowed to get our bearings. Our entrance into West Yellowstone increased our desire to close in on nature; the rustic panorama suggested that we probe deeper into its wilds. Gloria's thoughts mirrored mine as she glanced towards the clock on the dash. It was still early afternoon. She said, "Let's drive over to Madison Canyon. It's so beautiful and peaceful there, and the children can see the totem pole at the camp where we stayed before." The car wheeled north. We did not stop.

Our first vacation at Halford Camp in 1954. Photo courtesy of Gloria Roberts

Cynthia: My parents had fond memories of their last vacation in the majestic Madison Canyon at Halford Camp. It was tucked away along the Madison River below the Hebgen Lake Dam. The resort had a number of charming quaint cabins and a colorful totem pole in front of the cabin where guests checked in. It was a great place for a child to do some exploring. Halford Camp was the official name but Dad called it Halford's Camp.

Dad: *The trip around the lake to Hebgen Dam seemed much longer than I had remembered it. We dropped into the seven-mile canyon beyond the dam, and the further down we traveled, the higher the mountains on each side became. The canyon was beautifully arranged by nature. There was a blue-hued and winding stream. A pine-shrouded covering met with towering jagged cliffs below peaks capped with stone. And, there was an aura of peace that set the mood for its grandeur. No doubt about it, we opined, this place was to be our haven of rest. We had found it!*

Cynthia: Before we arrived at Halford Camp, we stopped at the store at Campfire Lodge. The owner of the store was outgoing and talkative. I was busy looking for a candy supply and not too attentive to the adult conversation, until the guy started talking about a grizzly bear he discovered going through his dumpster. At that point, I strained to hear him talk. He shot at the bear and was almost certain that he wounded it. The man spun a dramatic tale of a fierce and angry grizzly ready to attack at any moment. He warned us to be extra careful and to be "wounded bear aware." I decided that exploring was now off of my list and fishing was back on. I wanted to be close to Dad for protection.

Dad and Cynthia by the Madison River in 1954. Photo courtesy
of Gloria Roberts.

Chapter Two

Arrival at Halford Camp

Dad: *We arrived at Halford's Camp, and the children took to it immediately. The varnished totem pole in front of the camp, the colored stones lying about, the little chipmunks dashing for shelter, the bridge over the tributary stream, and the mountain flowers all promised fun. This day would be among our souvenirs. Hank Powers, who owned Halford's Camp, led us to a cabin about fifty yards from the river. Inside we were greeted by a neat and comfortable room. The two large beds at the far end of the room appeared soft as haystacks and reminded me how tired I was from the trip. "Where is the best fishing now, Hank?" I inquired. "I would say down by Rock Creek," he replied. "Good," I said, "I'll try it tomorrow."*

Cynthia: My mother was not certain that a cabin would be available at Halford Camp because it was so popular during the summer. It was the height of the tourist season. She was delighted when she discovered that one of the nicer cabins was not booked. We were assigned to a cozy little

6

place. It seemed small compared to the cabins of today, which are actually vacation homes. There was a little porch by the front door leading into a rustic kitchen. At the other end, were two double beds situated at either side of the back door. Nancy insisted on sleeping across from our parents. I was to sleep close to the window and against the sturdy log wall. There was a nail pounded in the log above my place, and my sister hung her ball cap there. I remember arguing with her about it because I did not want it hovering over my head in the dark. To my dismay, she got her way once again. The thought of the wounded grizzly bear was etched firmly in my brain. We heard squirrels chattering and running around. Nancy and I decided to go outside to check things out. We stuck close to the cabin. As we watched the overly active squirrels and chipmunks, we also noticed that the birds were wildly flying around. A wounded bird was on the ground nearby. We wanted to nurse it back to health, but our parents told us to leave it alone and to let nature take care of its own.

Dad: *Towards evening, we took a walk downstream to take in the canyon's beauty. We were nervous, however, because we had heard that there was a wounded bear in the area. We decided to return to our cabin and retire for the night.*

Cynthia: Another reason that we went for a walk along the river was because my dad wanted to find the rock he fished from the last time we were there. He enjoyed fishing from that rock and was anxious to locate it. When he spotted it, he was so excited. We intended to return to the rock and fish from it sometime during the week. Mom told me that he was determined to try his luck at Rock Creek first, as Hank Powers had suggested. He was ready to go catch fish as soon as the sun was up. We returned to the cabin with a resolution to go to bed and get up early. As we were getting ready for bed, my mother turned on the faucet over the kitchen sink. She was overcome by a sulfur-like smell. She insisted that my dad inspect it. He said he did not smell anything. After that, she started to stack suitcases on chairs in front of each door. She, too, was worried about that grouchy bear. It never occurred to me that the bear would storm the cabin. Now, I was even more anxious but grateful that my sister was the one closest to the door. My mother put her wedding rings on top of a sturdy round oak table sitting in the middle of the room and my father placed his watch there, as well. I gazed out of the window for a moment. It was a gorgeous moonlit night. I blinked at the ball cap and closed my eyes.

Dad: *The children were in their bed when I jumped into mine. There were two doors in the cabin, one at each end. Gloria was busily putting a chair up to each door. There were no locks so I assumed that this was to be our protection. As she began placing luggage on the chairs I inquired as to what she was doing. Looking concerned, but confident, she answered, "If either of these chairs starts moving, we'll know a bear is coming in and we can head for the opposite door." I gave a smirk, but my mind, refusing to carry the joke further, covered itself with a blanket of sleep.*

Dad, Dean Roberts, fishing on the Madison River in 1954. Photo courtesy of Gloria Roberts.

Chapter 3

Night Terror

Cynthia: Suddenly, my eyes popped wide open as I heard the back door rattle. It was 11:37 p.m., as I was told later. I wondered why that bear picked our cabin, of all the cabins in this valley, to break into. "Mommy, can you hear that?" I asked, poking my head above my slumbering sister. My mother must have heard it about the same time because she was trying to wake my father.

Dad: A sound, beginning with a low weak murmur, penetrated my senses. I felt a touch on my arm. I awoke to a mystery. There was a strange air about the place. Now the sound became scratchy like a large animal was pawing at the cabin. "There is a bear out there!" Gloria said. "Oh, no!" I thought out loud, as if the joke were on me. The door between our beds began to open, pushing the chair before it. Then it hit. The entire cabin began to wrench and heave.

Cynthia: My mother was disoriented after waking up in

a dark and unfamiliar place. She also described the sound as scratching and pawing on the screen door. At first, she thought it was a bear. When she snapped out of her haze, she immediately knew that it was an earthquake.

Both doors opened as the rattling continued. Not even the chairs with the suitcases could prevent that from happening. I surmised that the bear must have had some buddies. Soon, the entire cabin began to rock back and forth. Chinking from the logs rained down on us. I heard all sorts of things crashing to the floor. My sister fell out of bed. I grabbed her arms. "Hang on, Nancy, and I'll pull you back up!" I screamed. She did not seem to hear me. I was determined to pull her back onto the bed. With all of the strength within me, I yanked her back up and held her tight from that point on. We had no idea what was happening to our parents on the other bed. Even though they were close by, it was too dark to see them and too loud to hear them from all of the commotion and the growling of the earth.

Dad: *Objects flew at us in the dark. Cupboards, pans and dishes were all over, grinding and smashing violently. A forty-gallon water tank and a large iron stove hit the floor simultaneously. The logs of the cabin squealed and groaned. Terror gripped my heart and panic seized me. Though I knew that my wife was beside me in bed, I had no idea what was happening to the children. "My babies! My babies!" came Gloria's cry.*

Cynthia: Mother believed that she would never see her children again. She was frightened and despondent because she felt responsible for us being there. A large cupboard filled with dishes plummeted to the floor. She heard the water tank rolling back and forth over the smashed glass.

The shaking subsided a bit and our dad jumped on top of us. He asked if we were okay. My naïve self did not comprehend that this was all due to a force of nature.

11

Dad: *I hurled myself across my wife and landed on a bouncing floor. My sudden action sharpened my senses. I realized that it must be an earthquake. Reaching their bed, I felt for the children. I found them. I had to get to the doorway before the roof caved in. I had a child under each arm and had started to lift them off the bed, when I heard the loudest sound I have ever heard. The shaking became even more violent. I was forced face down on the bed across the children. I was frozen in place by a gigantic force. A terrific pressure opened the front door and blasted into the cabin. I thought it was the end of the world!*

Cynthia: Soon after my dad leaped onto our bed, a loud crack resounded in the night air. It was like the crackling of lightening only 10,000 times louder. In a few seconds, I heard an even louder sound. It was a thundering explosion! It threw our cabin back into commotion. My mother describes it as a "horrible rumbling, deafening and surreal sound." The rocking and reeling began again as a mighty wind blew through the doors. I wondered, "Will it ever stop?"

Dad *"How could this thing last so long without ripping the world apart?" I thought. It was then that the cabin fell from its foundation and tilted up on an angle. The shaking began to subside; it was minutes since it had begun. Outside a woman was screaming and weeping. I heard water running. "Let's get out of here, quick!" I exclaimed. "The river must have changed course!"*

Cynthia: Even though the violent shaking had stopped, the earth was still moaning and quivering. I could hear someone screaming and crying outside. Later, my mother learned that the desperate cries came from a teenage girl hired to clean the cabins for a summer job. The Powers were teachers in Idaho during the winter months. The girl was one of their students and she was staying alone in one of the

12

units. I sat up on my bed and tried to look out of the window to see where the hysterical sound was coming from. The moon was hiding behind a thick cloud of dirt-filled air. I saw nothing.

Dad: The back door was jammed shut. Some moonlight was coming through the front door, and I started toward it, I could see that it, too, was partly jammed. Because of the tilt of the cabin, I was moving up hill. I was not cautious as I plowed over broken glass and other debris in my effort to reach the door. My bare unsure feet found a watery surface. I fell, lunging forward, crashing my head against the fallen water tank. I fought unconsciousness hard. Gloria called to me. I was able to get to my feet and to the door.

Outside, the moon illuminated the air, which was heavily laden with dust. "Landslide!" a voice screamed. I could hear the sound of rocks crashing down from all directions.

Parked by the side of the cabin was my car, apparently undamaged. All around it the ground was crumpled like a wadded newspaper. Jagged rocks protruded from the injured earth, resembling fractured bones, and water oozed like blood from its wounds. Inside our cabin I could see the searching ray of a flashlight. Gloria had found the one, which I had put under my pillow before going to bed. I entered the cabin with one thought, to get my family and flee!

Cynthia: "We need to get out of here," my dad yelled. He went first to see what we were dealing with. By the time he returned, my mother was ready to leave. Dad told us to carefully walk out to the car because there was broken glass and water all over the floor. Mom was worried that we were experiencing flooding from the river, but it was the water heater gushing all over the room.

Dad: Back inside the cabin I was met by Cynthia who shouted, "Has he gone daddy? Has the bear gone?" Little Nancy said nothing.

Snatching the flashlight from Gloria, I swept the cabin with its beam. There were four bare walls, mute effigies of the havoc which had hit them. The floor was a garbage dump, strewn with food and broken objects. The stove, its pipe twisted and splintered, was lying lidless before a sink covered with broken glass. The tank lay prone as water dripped from its belly. The cabin smelled like a swamp. Neatness and comfort had left the place.

My wrist watch lay at my feet: the crystal was broken; most of the pins were shaken out of the band's joining links; the hands were stopped, indicating 11:46. As I scooped it up, I recalled having bought it in Zermatt, Switzerland. I had wound it for the first time while in Bern — the day an earthquake hit that city.

Cynthia: Mom grabbed her wedding rings from off of the table as we left. During the quake, her rings simply bounced up and down without falling off.

Dad: *I found my trousers, and fortunately, the keys to the car were in them. My other personal effects were scattered somewhere in the debris. Gloria was barking orders like a first sergeant, telling me which things to find and take with us. I forced her to leave, and we all piled into the car in our pajamas.*

Cynthia: Thanks to our mother's bear preparation, the suitcases were easy to find on the chairs near the doors. We grabbed them and tried to tip toe over broken glass and running water. Mom looked for her favorite sweater in order to cover her firmly fitting and flimsy pajamas. She discovered it pinned underneath the water heater. She yanked on the sweater until it was freed, but it ended up dotted with large holes. Arriving first at the car, I noticed that it was no longer locked. The shaking had unlocked all four doors! Some people were out of their cabins and making plans to leave. For the first time I heard the word "earthquake." In fact, my vocabulary was about to expand a great deal in the next 24 hours. As my parents and others were deciding what to do, I thought it might be a good idea to pray. I walked back in the direction of the cabin to find a private place to kneel down. I found a spot and I sunk to my knees. I could feel the earth rumbling beneath me. It felt like kneeling on a plate of groaning gelatin. I jumped up quickly and said a short prayer on my feet. My parents were not happy that I had wandered off. Even Nancy remembers me disappearing and getting reprimanded. They had visuals of me tumbling off of a ledge or the earth swallowing me up. Later, I realized that some of my parent's fears were not unfounded.

Chapter 4

Trapped

Dad: *I pulled the car up on the road not knowing where to head from there. Headlights flashed on to our front—the Powers were preparing to leave. I leaped from my car and ran towards Hank, who was now coming my way. "Let's go!" he called out. "The dam might not hold!*

The dam! I had forgotten! A new terror gripped me; we were in a direct channel below it. We would have to get to higher ground. I pulled up behind the Power's car, and as I did so, others in the camp joined in, forming a caravan. We crossed the bridge by the camp and headed downstream. We did not get very far, for it appeared that the whole mountain had fallen into the canyon. We circled back towards the dam, using a road, which was higher up on the mountain. Our progress was slow because the road had many rocks on it and was lined with cracks. The larger openings were examined before cars proceeded. Cars and trailers were coming from two directions. We were cut off from both sides. The road was jammed with people, none knowing what to do.

16

Cynthia: As the cabin dwellers tried to drive out of the area, I felt a sense of relief. We crawled along the badly cracked road for a short distance before being stopped by people in other cars. We were told that part of a mountain had slid and buried the road. Now we knew what caused that horrible cracking and explosive sound during the earthquake! Hope was still alive. There was one other way out of the canyon. As soon as we turned around in the opposite direction, we were stopped again. We were told that portions of the road had dropped off into the lake down by the dam. There was no way out. We were trapped in earthquake canyon!

The sense of relief that I once felt turned into panic. I wondered how and if we would ever get out of there alive. My mother continued to cry and pray out loud. My dad echoed her prayers. Some of the people on the road reported seeing huge waves (seiches) sloshing back and forth over the dam. It was crucial to find the highest point to park our cars for the night in case the dam gave way. Mom told me that we followed Hank Powers to a place people used as a dumping ground for unwanted items such as old bedsprings. Back in those days, the road was slightly above the area so that cars could drive into it. Now, the road is below it and the only way to get to it is by foot. This place became known as "Refuge Point."

Dad: *One of the men among us, who knew the canyon well, informed us that we were now on ground which should be safe if the dam broke. We pulled off the road into an area clear of trees but covered with brush. Our only choice was to wait this thing out. The ground beneath us was in a continued state of unrest. There was one jar after another, but the worst was the report that the dam was going out. All night we waited while others found their way into our makeshift camp. Some were injured; some were separated from their families; some were without clothing; some*

17

had lost their cars and trailers; all had a story to tell. Dark clouds rolled over bringing lightning, thunder, and rain. The people of our camp responded with clothing and shelter for those in need. It was a long night.

Cynthia: Not long after we parked our car, the moon disappeared behind thick clouds. As it began to thunder and lightening, it reminded me of the terrible sounds that rocked our world earlier in the night. I imagined that it was heaven weeping as the rain descended upon us. The sound of screams and cries for help bounced off canyon walls from injured and trapped people. Someone knocked on our window and asked if a man and his small daughter could spend the night with us. The rest of their family was divided up among the other vehicles. Their car was swept away when fierce winds and violent waves swooped through the canyon after the landslide. They were soaking wet and had nothing but their pajamas and a blanket that was given to them. The little stranger next to me eventually nodded off to sleep. I stared blankly out of the window and listened to the rain as it tapped on the roof of our car. I could not sleep as I impatiently waited for the light of day.

Dad: Sleepless eyes welcomed the dawn. The once carefree faces, some now stained with blood, were grim and expressionless. Shock was evident everywhere as experiences were exchanged. The beautiful canyon of yesterday was the wreckage of today. On one end millions of tons of earth and rock had plopped itself down, like a giant chunk of biscuit dough, blocking it completely. A dam had been made in seconds, which would have taken many years to complete. On one side of the dam a lake was building, and on the other was the practically dry streambed. There was no telling how many people were buried beneath this alter of sacrifice, which now lay like a piece of molten lava. Up by the Hebgen Dam, the road was missing as if a giant hammer had smacked into it causing it to fall into the icy depths of the lake. Frothy orange water flowed from the cliffs, which had been cracked and split. Looking up at the peaks, I could see the horizon move as the aftershocks continued. The cracking of the rocks echoed and re-echoed across the canyon as pieces fell to the floor below in puffs of dust. Running through the trees in all directions were vein-like fissures. We were seasick from standing on this island of motion.

Dad said the Madison Slide looked like "a giant chunk of biscuit dough." This photo is also on the back cover. Credit U.S. Geological Survey.

Red Canyon fault scarp and fissures running through the ground east of Blarneystone Ranch. Photo credit U.S. Geological Survey

Road damage caused an accident when someone tried to escape the quake area. Photo credit U.S. Geological Survey.

Another view of the road damage. Photo credit U.S. Geological Survey.

Cynthia: By the first rays of dawn, the survivors were up and busy at work. Most of us had nothing to eat, while some had food and gas stoves. Everyone came together in a common cause and shared what little provisions they had with the group. They served coffee and breakfast to those that were interested. The majority remained calm and level headed. Someone started a fire and invited the children to come warm themselves. We were told that one of the purposes of the fire was to send smoke signals to planes. I walked down in my pajamas to the fire to be with the other children. Because I was alone and did not know anyone, I mostly observed what was going on around me. I did not talk or play any games like some of the rest of the kids. As soon as a plane was seen in the distance, some of the adults tried to send smoke signals. In spite of their feeble attempt, the plane spotted us anyway. It came closer and circled our little camp. We all yelled and waved. After that, planes continued to fly by. My Mom tells me that an amateur radio operator communicated with a pilot from one of the planes.

The pilot insisted that we get to higher ground because if the dam broke, we would be "goners."

At one point, while we were gathered around the fire, a woman asked us to close our eyes for a few minutes. I was too curious and squinted as I pretended to close my eyes. As I was peeking, I saw her throw bright red rags into the flames. I noticed that the older boy sitting next to me watched her intently. I found the courage to ask him what the woman was doing. "She is burning bloody rags from the injured," he announced.

My heart sank. Up until that moment, I was thinking only about myself. I thought of this as a huge, scary inconvenience. We were okay. We had survived with only a few bumps, scrapes and bruises. Everyone that I could visibly see seemed fine. However, there was unimaginable pain and suffering going on that I was obviously unaware of. Even though we were okay, it did not stop me from experiencing complete and utter fear. I believed that there was a good possibility we were all going to die anyway, injured or not. As the day progressed, we heard some touching stories that would haunt our lives forever.

My mother and Nancy stayed in the car for a while. Mom was embarrassed to be seen in her clingy pajamas. Coincidentally, the Searcy family that bought our house in Salt Lake City was camping at Beaver Creek when the quake hit. They put up a tent at Refuge Point and invited my mother to use it to change her clothes. That proved to be a game changer for her. She was now able to walk around and visit with other survivors.

Refuge Point during an aftershock. Notice the dust stirred up by boulders crashing down the mountainside. Dad is walking in front touching his hat. Our 1959 Mercury is on the left and Mom is in the front seat. Photo courtesy of John Owen, Halford Camp Survivor.

The place our car was parked at Refuge Point. Personal photo,
2009

Chapter 5

Discovered

Dad: A plane came over the area and dropped a message. We were instructed to collect all the injured for evacuation by helicopter. Everyone pitched in to help where they could.

Six fire fighters from Missoula, Montana, parachuted into the area. Their brightly colored chutes were their banners of courage. When the helicopters came and landed on a clearing, which we had made for them, they brought a doctor and two nurses. It had been at least twelve hours since the injured had waited for medical help and the evacuation began. The Air Force brought in tents, food and water.

Cynthia: It was a spectacular thing to see. The sky was filled with the colorful parachutes of smoke jumpers and boxes of food floating from above. They came to assist the injured and to facilitate our rescue. Mom said that they had plans in case we were there for a while. If we had to stay, they were going to set up tents in separate areas for the men and the women for privacy purposes.

Forest Service smoke jumper. Personal photo, 2009.

Fortunately, there were two nurses staying in the area at the time of the quake. They did all that they could to help save lives, with hardly any medical supplies. After the injured were evacuated by helicopter, they were taken to West Yellowstone and eventually flown to a hospital in Bozeman, Montana.

Dad: During our stay in the area the most difficult item to get in was news. The entire period was one of expectancy. We kept vigil for another big quake or the dam to go out. Our condition was summed up by the action of a woman when she collapsed to the ground in tears—she could stand no more.

Cynthia: My mother remembers the woman, Polly Weston, my dad referred to. She cried out as she sat on the ground, "I just can't take this anymore!" She and her husband, Hal, were vacationing with their two nephews Billy and Steve. Both nephews disappeared sometime during the day. We all tried to find them, but they were nowhere to be seen. This was the last straw for Aunt Polly. One of the nephews, Bill Conley, told us exactly what they were up to when he spoke at the 50th commemorative anniversary of the quake. The two boys were off exploring and taking home movies. Bill was kind enough to mail the survivors a copy of his earthquake adventures after the reunion. The boys got some great footage of the smoke jumpers, fault scarps, road damage and the helicopters that came to evacuate the injured.

Dad: *Planes carrying newspapermen, representing papers from all over the country, circled the area. There were so many planes overhead at one time that the reverberations of the motors were triggering slides of loose rocks. Some newsmen came in for on-the-spot interviews and pictures. We now knew that we were big news to the entire nation.*

Cynthia: Information was delivered through the grapevine. We tried to find out how the injured were doing. I remember hearing about a few of them. Adults tried to shelter the children from that kind of news, but I knew that the blood-soaked rags came from individuals with critical injuries. News circulated about people who were camping close to the slide. Many of them were hurt by falling rock and debris. The two nurses set up areas to attend to them in the back of vehicles and trailers. I do recall an older couple. They clung to a tree all night, surrounded by a rising lake of cold water. Mom remembers hearing their desperate calls for help all night and into the early morning hours. It is a horrible and frustrating feeling when someone needs help and there is no way to get to them. Fortunately, the couple was eventually rescued. They were brought back shivering and trembling, wrapped in thick blankets, and placed in a station wagon. Later, we learned that their last name was Mault.

I was interested in everyone's earthquake story. I hung out with Dad during the day and listened as he visited with people. A man in the camp told Dad an intriguing story. He and his family drove into the canyon about 11:30 p.m. They were tired and weary from driving. They stopped at the Rock Creek Campground hoping to stay for the night. When they were informed that the campground was filled to capacity and that they could not stay, they decided to pull over somewhere to rest for a while. The area was lined with cars and trailers and there was no place to park. The family was not happy as they continued on their journey. A few minutes later, the car became difficult to steer and they wondered if they had a flat tire. They could not believe their streak of bad luck. As they were deciding what to do, the man glanced into his rear view mirror just in time to witness the mountain crashing down! They were seconds away from being buried alive under a mass of rock and earth.

Mom recalls another close call told to her by a different family. As they drove in from the east by the dam, they also experienced difficulty steering their car. Suddenly, the road dropped into the lake right in back of them. They barely missed sinking into the water.

Large alcove on the north shore of Hebgen Lake where Highway 287 slumped into the water. Photo credit U.S. Geological Survey.

Where the road once was. Photo credit U.S. Geological Survey.

My mom was sad when she heard about what happened to the mother and adult disabled son vacationing in the cabin next to us. He had a form of paraplegia and it was difficult for him to move, especially when he got excited. The Powers were convinced that we were all accounted for when we drove out of Halford Camp after the quake. It is easy to get confused, forgetful and disoriented in a situation like that. With great difficulty, the woman helped her son out to their car. Somehow, they were able to find their way to Refuge Point. Everyone, especially the Powers, felt

29

terrible that they were left behind.

In the morning, Mr. Powers asked my dad to go back with him to the cabins to retrieve some medicine that was badly needed by the disabled man. The mountain slide had blocked the river and the water was quickly building up. It would not be long until the water covered the cabins. The night before, we were willing to leave it all behind. I asked my dad if it was necessary for him to go back. He assured me that everything would be fine. Nancy wanted Dad to go get her ball cap. In fact, she wanted to go with him, but that was not going to happen. As we watched the two men walk away, we were on pins and needles until they returned. It seemed like it took forever. They reported that it was a disaster inside of the cabins and it was hard to find things. Luckily, they were able to retrieve the disabled man's medicine. Dad went back to our tilted garbage dump of a cabin. He wrapped a few things in a sheet that he pulled off of one of the beds. Later, Mother wished he had grabbed her tablecloth instead of the sheet because it had been a wedding gift. My dad found Nancy's ball cap still hanging on the nail above where I had slept. Yes, it was still hanging there while everything else was in shambles on the floor!

During the day, there was one continual aftershock after another. Some of these were strong and caused rock slides. We watched big boulders tumbling down the mountains, kicking up the dirt as they bounced along the way. With each aftershock, I prayed that the dam would hold. I tried to distract myself by taking pictures with my black box camera. There was a treasure trove of photos waiting to be developed. I had to do some hiking in order to relieve myself. It was hard to hide from the prying eyes of at least 200 people. To make matters worse, both Dad and I were experiencing intestinal problems. All the emotions went right to the gut. On the way back from a potty break with Mom and Nancy, I tripped and dropped the camera. The film popped out of the back of it and my photos were doomed from the exposure of the sun. My parents were in too much shock to care about taking any pictures. At the time, we had no visual evidence that we were actually there. Thanks to survivors like John Owen, who snapped some incredible pictures and were willing to share them, we now have evidence.

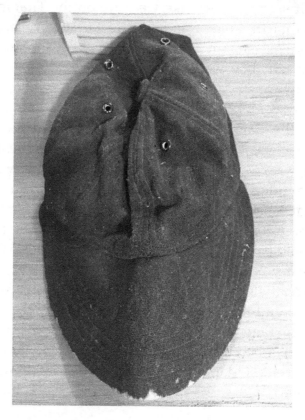

Nancy still has her ball cap. Photo courtesy of Nancy Roberts, 2017.

There was uncertainty as to what was to become of our new tribe. Rumors began to float around the camp. At one point, we heard that the rescuers were going to evacuate women and children by helicopter and the men would stay behind. It started to feel like we were on the Titanic. There was talk that the dam was about to burst. We heard that towns down stream such as Ennis, Montana, were evacuated. If they were evacuated, we realized that there was no way we stood a chance. A nice man tried to alleviate our concerns. His grandfather was one of the engineers that designed the dam back in 1914. He assured us that his grandfather was a perfectionist throughout his life and that the dam was well built and sturdy enough to withstand almost anything. A picture of an old marker near the dam stated that when it was constructed, it was 721 feet long, 87 feet high, 6,500 feet above sea level and was made of concrete and earth-fill. The reservoir contained 345,000 acre-feet of water and was said to be one of the largest in the world at that elevation. The dam's purpose was for power production and it was owned and operated by the Montana Power Company. Whenever I heard concerns about the dam, I remembered the man talking about his grandfather and how well the dam was built. It helped me to have faith that it would hold.

Hebgen Dam after the 1959 earthquake. Note the curve in the concrete core. Photo credit U.S. Geological Survey.

Damage to the Hebgen Dam spillway. Photo credit U.S.
Geological Survey.

Refuge Point, August 18, 1959. Photo courtesy of John Owen, Halford Camp Survivor

Landslide that destroyed part of highway 287 by Hebgen Lake.
Photo credit U.S. Geological Survey

Chapter 6

Escaping

Cynthia: We heard that a road construction crew with several bulldozers had arrived from Butte, Montana. They started digging an emergency dirt road so that we could escape to the east by the dam. There was no promise as to when it would be completed. These brave men worked feverishly throughout the day during tremors and rockslides. They did not care about their own safety. They put the lives of others first. There were numerous people making sacrifices on our behalf. They were the helpers. When Fred Rogers, well known for his children's television program, "Mr. Rogers' Neighborhood" was a child, his wise mother told him what to watch for in times of tragedy, "Look for the helpers. You will always find people who are helping." Mr. Rogers went on to say, "If you look for the helpers, you'll know there is hope." Our helpers were our heroes. They gave us hope.

Dad: Some time after 6 p.m. the word came to us that

construction crews had worked tirelessly all day to cut a road
around the side of the mountain by the lake. We could leave!

Our camp took on the appearance of a land rush as we tore
down tents, picked up our equipment, and loaded our cars. Time
was taken to say good-bye to new friends, the ones who would be
remembered, probably not by their names, but by their faces and
experiences. As I drove to safety, I tried to take inventory of my
losses; it made me ashamed, for I had the comforting knowledge
that my family was among the survivors. (End of Dad's account)

Cynthia: Excitement filled the air when we heard news
that the crew finished the emergency road. It was
unbelievable that they had accomplished this task in such a
short period of time. The Red Cross prepared a place for all
of us in a dormitory at Montana State College (Montana
State University) in Bozeman, Montana. Although it was out
of our way, we were determined to go there for support. It
seemed like it took an eternity before we were escorted out
of the canyon. The Red Cross gave us sandwiches before we
left. Mom said that they were the best sandwiches that she
had ever tasted. I could not eat a sandwich. My appetite
was gone. As we left Refuge Point, the cars crawled like
snails over the badly torn road. There was a great deal of
stopping and starting along the way. We passed the road
crew. They were sweaty and grimy from head to toe. We
waved and thanked them as we drove by. We could see the
devastation to the landscape. Fissures covered the earth.
There was not much left of the road by the lake. It only took
about a minute, the longest minute of my life, to destroy this
majestic and gorgeous place.

**Note the new road that was dug for the survivors to escape.
Credit U.S. Geological Survey**

The sun was going down when we reached the dam. We had to stop there for a while as it took time for cars to pass through the roughly hewn temporary road. We were astonished at the damage done to the dam's spillway. It did not look the same. The lake had tilted and dropped during the quake. The north shore was eight feet higher and the south shore was eight feet lower. In spite of it all, the well-constructed dam remained strong. The man who told us about his grandfather was correct. In 1976, when I was in Sugar City, Idaho, helping clean up after the Teton Dam disaster, my thoughts returned to the Hebgen Lake Dam. When I saw the ruin left behind by the failed Teton Dam, I was forever grateful that the dam in Madison Canyon was constructed properly. "Thank you," brilliant engineers and wonderful construction workers from the past!

**Large crack in the concrete retaining wall of Hebgen Dam.
Credit U.S. Geological Survey.**

The cars drove out first and bulldozers pulled out the trailers last. It was a huge relief to drive away from that dam! Fear melted away as the sun's last rays evaporated. It was pitch black. According to my mom, all the cars were identified and registered as we left. Cars belonging to rescuers were stationed at different points along the route. They flashed their lights as we passed so that we could see where we were going. Our vehicles were counted each time we passed the lit up cars in order to make sure we were still together. Our family had anxiety because we were moving so slowly, especially my father due to the fact that our gas tank was almost empty. This was yet another complicated twist to our journey. We realized we had to find a gas station soon! Who knew what would happen if we ran out of gas. The thought of staying in that area another night was torture. Tension was high until we found a gas station. It was at this time that my dad vowed to never let the car get below half a tank again. He kept this promise for the remaining 50 years of his life.

We were now lagging behind the caravan. Our lonely car drove to Bozeman through thick darkness. We were the last to arrive at the shelter provided for the survivors. They were expecting us. When we walked in, a woman from the Red Cross exclaimed to Mother, "You are the last ones in!"

My dad was sent to the men's section of the dormitory and my sister and I went with my mom to the women's section. My mother recalls being upset about the separation in the dorms. She did not want any of us out of her sight! The room was filled with bunk beds and cots. Most people were already asleep. We found an empty bunk and my sister curled up with my mom on the bottom bed. I refused to go up to the top. Before this experience, I would have jumped at the chance to get the top bunk. My mom did not argue with me, and the three of us squished together on the narrow mattress.

In the morning, we went over to the cafeteria. The Red Cross provided a wonderful breakfast but I refused to eat it. My appetite was still non-existent. We sat with the disabled man and his mother and enjoyed visiting with them.

There were reporters from local newspapers from Salt Lake City and national magazines that came to interview us. A newspaper reporter visited with my parents. He asked if there was anyone back home that we wanted him to contact. There were a few neighbors that knew we were gone, but no relatives. My mom suggested that he call my grandmother. My maternal grandmother got the call and was surprised to hear that we were gone, let alone survivors of one of the biggest earthquakes our nation had ever experienced. She was stressed about other things going on in her life at the time and did not understand what the reporter was trying to tell her. She thought that he said that my father and his daughters survived. Family members and friends read the list of the survivors in the newspaper and it, too, was not clear. First of all, our last name was recorded as "Robert" instead of "Roberts." They listed our names, but not my mother's. Everyone back home questioned whether or not she survived.

The reporters from newspapers and national magazines were friendly, but they were looking for the big scoop. We did not have a horrific personal tragedy or exciting rescue. When the story was not dramatic enough, they would literally back away from us. A reporter from *Life* magazine tripped over Nancy while doing just that. He was built like a linebacker and worried that he had injured her. She was toughened by the last few days and simply brushed it off as if nothing had happened. Nancy explained it this way, "I don't know why this big guy with the microphone only wanted to talk to Mom and Dad. I accidentally got behind him because I was certain he wanted to talk to me. No, I made him fall over instead. However, he thought he had hurt me when he fell and I got a nickel out of it! Not bad, even though no interview was recorded with me."

Another reporter gave us girls a carton of chocolate milk. Nancy was excited to take the drink. She had been eating cold bean soup right from the can at Refuge Point. To her, it was all part of the adventure. Chocolate milk was usually a real treat for me, but I could not stomach the thought of drinking it. When I declined, my mother took the milk and apologized on my behalf and scolded me for not being gracious and polite.

A longitudinal step fault scarp, part of the Hebgen Fault on Mount Hebgen, about a half a mile from Hebgen Dam. Photo credit U.S. Geological Survey

Chapter 7

Going Home

We were finally able to leave and started to work our way back home. Because of the road damage in West Yellowstone, we returned to Utah from a different direction. Besides, the thought of going anywhere near the quake area was troubling. Our journey took us to Star Valley, Wyoming, where we stayed overnight. During the night, there was a thunderstorm. Mom said that the roof of the place that we stayed at was made of tin. The raindrops sounded like baseballs as they pounded down upon the roof. My sister and I were now officially terrified of thunder and lightening. On our way back, we listened to the interviews of the survivors on the radio. Lightening struck overhead and our car radio went silent. Our parents never did hear their own interview. Neighbors back home listening to the interview were relieved to hear Gloria's voice and to realize that she had survived.

Cynthia and Nancy on the way home, August 19, 1959. Photo courtesy of Gloria Roberts

We were all looking forward to our return home and we were overjoyed when our car finally pulled into our carport, but I felt numb inside. Even at a young age, I sensed that my life would never be quite the same. Everyone was happy that we returned. Both of my grandmothers were excited to see us. We became celebrities for a few weeks. It was overwhelming to repeat the story over and over again. My paternal grandmother mended my mom's favorite sweater and life went on as usual. I wanted to forget that it had ever happened.

We continued to pray for the injured. When we learned that quake victims, Margaret Holmes and Myrtle Painter died from their injuries, we were heart broken. We had high hopes that all of the injured would survive.

We bought all of the magazines and books about the

quake that were available at the time. My dad wrote his memoirs in December of 1959. It was unbelievable to think that we had been part of this historical event. There were 28 people that lost their lives as a result of the earthquake and 19 of them were buried under the slide. Five drowned when ferocious winds and displaced water overtook them west of the slide. Two individuals perished when a boulder landed on their tent at the Cliff Lake Campground, and two others died from their injuries at a hospital in Bozeman. The Rock Creek Campground was at capacity that night and it was partially buried by the landslide. My mother believes there may be other victims underneath the rock and earth that were never reported missing.

In 1999, mountain climbers discovered some remains on Granite Peak, Montana's tallest mountain. A year later, other climbers found more remains in the same area. They were tested and found to belong to the same person. It is possible that the bones were exposed because of snowmelt resulting from hot summers and mild winters. There was speculation that the remains were those of Ernest Bruffey, a hiker that registered at the Summit on August 16, 1959, the day before the quake. He vanished and was not heard from again. Some believed that he was buried under a rockslide caused by the quake and was actually the 29th casualty of the earthquake. The condition of the remains, as well as the fact that they were found out in the open, is evidence that the person fell while descending from the peak. Why it happened, and who the person really was has not been confirmed. It is still a mystery.

Memorial boulder and plaque dedicated to those who lost their lives as a result of the 1959 Hebgen Lake Earthquake. Author photo from 2009.

Sydney D.A. Ballard, Margaret Ballard, Christopher T. Ballard, Purley R. Bennett, Tom O. Bennett, Carole Bennett, Susan Bennett, Bernie L. Boynton, Inez D. Boynton, Merle M. Edgerton M.D., Edna M. Edgerton, Margaret D. Holmes, Myrtle L. Painter, Roger G. Provost, Elizabeth F. Provost, Richard Provost, David Provost, Thomas M. Stowe, Marilyn W. Stowe, Edgar H. Stryker, Ethel M. Stryker, Robert J. Williams, Edith C. Williams, Steven R. Williams, Michael J. Williams, Christy L. Williams, Harmon Woods, Edna M. Woods.

Halford Camp Cabins floating away with the rest of the debris.
Photo courtesy U.S. Geological Survey.

Chapter 8

Living With Survivors Guilt and Post Traumatic Stress Disorder (PTSD)

After we returned home from the 1959 Hebgen Lake Earthquake, we would reflect back on this terrifying experience. We made it out with our lives, vehicle and most of our belongings. We were fortunate.

At first we asked "what if" questions:

> What if we had camped in a tent instead of staying in a cabin?
> What if the cabin was not built as sturdy as it was?
> What if the logs had fallen on us, or the roof caved in?
> What if the mountain that fractured was the one in back of us instead of a short distance down the canyon?
> What if we had been injured?
> What if planes had not spotted us?
> What if good people like the Forest Service smoke

jumpers had not come to rescue us?
What if the temporary road had not been built?

Then there were the "why" questions:

Why did we have to go through this experience?
Why did we deserve this?
Why did we leave on vacation in the first place?
Why did we decide to go to the Madison River Canyon instead of staying in West Yellowstone?
Why did we not recognize the signs that an earthquake was eminent, like the animals being overly active and sulfur gas coming from the pipe in the kitchen sink?
Why did we survive and others did not?

Survivors ask these kinds of questions and they often live with the guilt of surviving.

Another quote from one of my favorite people, Mr. Rogers, states: "No matter what children know about a "crisis," it's especially scary for children to realize that their parents are scared." It was easy to tell that our parents were just as frightened as we were. After the initial shock, however, they handled the situation in a calm and rational manner. Even though that was the case, the trauma of it all did have an impact. The first few months after we arrived home, I became much more quiet and reflective. It took time to snap out of it. During the following year, Nancy and I started to have asthma attacks. We were healthy and carefree children before this experience. We never knew if it was from allergies to our cat, breathing all of the dust from the Madison slide or from emotional trauma. Mom recalls that for several years her teeth would chatter whenever she would talk about the earthquake. It was like reliving the experience all over again.

Nancy's kindergarten teacher talked to her class about earthquakes and mentioned the Hebgen Lake Quake. Nancy raised her hand and told the class that she had been in that earthquake. The teacher snapped back at her saying, "No, you were not!" My sister told Mom when she got home from school and the teacher received a phone call. Nancy was famous for the balance of kindergarten.

Every time the lightening cracked and the thunder roared, my sister and I were frightened out of our minds. For a short time, we lived beneath the mountains of the Wasatch Front. Knowing that there was an extensive fault line running through the mountain range was terrifying. I would lay awake at night worrying about an earthquake and a mountain collapsing. Going through any canyon caused me to panic. Nancy suffered from separation anxiety. It was difficult for her when she started school. I tried to hide the phobic side of my personality. Looking back on it, we probably needed counseling. That was not something people did back then, especially my tough WWII veteran dad. He had fought on the front lines of battle and he still experienced trauma from the earthquake. Something changes in a person when they are responsible for other people's lives.

In my opinion, we were never emotionally the same. I suppose this is true for anyone who has experienced any kind of disaster, natural or man-made. There seems to be one disaster after another these days. I always have empathy for the survivors because I know how it must be for them. For me personally, I have tried to conquer anxiety, panic attacks and depression throughout my life. I have experienced two tornado warnings in South Dakota and Colorado, and a hurricane in Hawaii. When Mother Nature takes charge, hold on for the ride! These were frightening experiences but none could match the night of August 17, 1959, when an earthquake cracked open a mountain.

Just like the Madison Canyon bears the scars from the 1959 earthquake, the survivors have their own emotional scars as well.

The following is a list of the evacuees exactly as it appeared in the *Billings Gazette* in 1959. Our last name is starred to note a correction.

LIST OF QUAKE EVACUEES GIVEN
Some Addresses Said Unavailable

BOZEMAN (AP)--Here is a partial list of evacuees who left the southwest Montana earthquake zone by way of Dug Creek, Wyo., and Bozeman, Mont., obtained through the Red Cross, Montana Highway Patrol and the U.S. Forest Service:
(Addresses unavailable where not listed)
Caraway, West and wife, from Hebgen Dam.
McFarland, Gerald; wife and daughter, Salem, Ore.
Yaklish, A. J., Woodenville, Wash.
Thompson, Mike, Udall, Kan.
Maxwell, V., Jr.
Thompson, June; man, woman, daughter, and aunt.
Martin, A. F.
Davis, Mrs. Ben.
Drake, Miss Goldie.
Davis, B. W.
Tarlton, Miss.
Sanders, Leland L., wife, daughter, Ina Jean,
Roy, Utah.
Thomas, Mrs. David, three children, Nye, Mont.
Rogers, Mrs. Charles, three children,
Roundup, Mont.
Wood, Mrs. Ethel, son Harry, Salt Lake City, Utah.

Curtis, L. H. and wife, Pasadena, Calif.
Balack, Clarence M., wife, one small girl, mother-
in-law, Middleton, Mrs. Erma, Tucson, Ariz.
Blaydon, Richard, wife, North Hollywood, Calif.
Tovias, Louis; wife Kay, daughter Karen,
Akron, Ohio.
Lorenze, Mrs. Fred, Akron, Ohio.
Genderson, Gilbert, Bellevue, Wash.
Willie, James B., Tacoma, Wash.
Badoviwax, John; wife, two children, Seattle, Wash.
Burley, Robert; wife.
Goodnough, Jack; wife, three children,
Albion, Wash.
Wils, Wilfor; wife, four children,
Brigham City, Utah.
Davis, John B.; Carolyn, Pocatello, Idaho.
Wizel, Fred; wife, four children, Aberdeen, Wash.
Hudson, Charotta, Twin Falls, Idaho.
Rost, Eleanor.
Greenaway.
Kraeter, Eugene G.; wife, Jean, Concord, Mass.
Bernard, Hayward; wife, three sons,
Escondido, Calif.
Melchon.
Cooper, William E.
Webb, Glenn.
Engle, F. N., wife, Garden Grove, Calif.
*Robert W. Dean, wife, two children, Nancy,
Cynthia, Salt Lake City, Utah. (Roberts W. Dean, wife
Gloria)
Daea, John Sr., Great Falls, Mont.
Stranger, J. F. and Leo.
Triempower, E.
Buser, Jack; wife, Harrisburg, Penn.
Bateman, Rex; wife, Utah.

Hobeson, C. W.; wife, two boys, Estan and Gary.
Three Painter children, Ogden, Utah.
Own, O. B., Culver City, Calif.
Searcy, J. Spencer; wife, Don, Ralph, Lina,
Salt Lake City, Utah.
Potter, Robert; wife, son Barry, 122 Custer Ave.,
Billings, Mont.
Bacon, Rodney E.; wife Alice, Santa Ana, Calif.
Bowns, Mr. and Mrs. Terry Eugene, and Jo Ann,
Salt Lake City.
Plaga, Jean; Pat, Salt Lake City.
Staley, Dr. Elden D.; Barbara V., Richard E.,
Leland V., Jeanne, Claudia, Rock Springs, Wyo.
Weston, H. G. and Mrs. Weston, San Jose; two
nephews, Stephen and Billy Conley.
Olson, Mr. and Mrs. Bernie, Kent, Wash., four
children, John, Fred, Gloria and Joanne.
Vernon, Richard Lynn; Annebel, Coalville, Utah.
Blakley, Howard S.; Adline D., Cheryl L., Dale H.,
810 Connie Ave., Rock Springs, Wyo.
Nomura, Dr. Frank Shimpie; Francis, Connie, Kan.
Maeda, Frank S.; Dorothy, Los Angeles.
White, Warren Bruce; wife, Frederick, Ruth Ann,
Indianapolis, Ind.
Reppat, Leonard V.; wife, Topeka, Kan.
Davis, Charles; wife, Terry, Lake George, Colo.
Maxwell, Vern; wife, Steve, Kim,
State Center, Iowa.
Barton, Mrs. Tom, State Center, Iowa.
Burbank, August L.; wife, Susan, Richard, Eugene,
Louisa, Penelope, Melani, Brigham City, Utah.
Lavett, Tehdore Avery; wife, Salt Lake City.
Greene, Ray; wife, Steve, 2312 10th North,
Billings, Mont.
Kennedy, Larry, Dayton, Ohio.

Morse, Mrs., Salt Lake City, Utah.

Jensen, Mr., Salt Lake City, Utah.

Donny, Mr. and wife, Vandalia, Ohio.

Campbell, Clark O.; wife, Ross O., Cathy Jean,
Box 274, Lovell, Wyo.

Donaldson, Donald; wife, Canfield, Ohio.

Kreuger, Harold; wife, Polly, Bruce, Larry, Mary,
Montello, Wis.

McDonald, John; wife, St. Anthony, Idaho.

Holtsman, I. K.; wife, Carrollton, Ohio.

Walker, Norman; wife, Rickey, Christinie,
Pleasant Grove, Utah.

Kalmer, Lela, Lehi, Utah.

Rogerson, Charles, Roundup, Mont.

Thomas, David and Mrs., Nye, Mont., 3 children,
David Jr., Carol and Ann.

Mr. and Mrs. Chas. T. Rogers, Roundup, Mont.,
Charles, Sandra, Patty.

Grub, Calvin; wife, two children,
Gen. Del., Butte, Mont.

Meyers, Henry; wife, Zella, children, 306 9th St.
West, Billings, Mont.

Hoggan, Donald S.; wife, Salt Lake City, Utah.

Hamada, Minoru; wife, 2 children, Roy, Utah, also
2 other children, Dick Maeda, Los Angeles.

Danny Nomura, Roy, Utah.

Yemoto, Kiyoshi; wife, son, Fresno, Calif.

Sogihara, George; son.

Miller, Edward Raymond; wife, 2 children,
Denver, Colo.

Owen, Lawrence Terril; wife, Dorothy, son John,
Riverside, Calif.

Keith, Kenneth; wife, Harrisburg, Ill.

Vander Pluym, John; wife, 2 children, Decatur, Ill.

Donegan, Clifton and Gene, children,

Vandalia, Ohio.

Good, Frederick Arnold Jr; wife Doris, 4 sons, Frederick, Robert, Alex, Jeff., La Canada, Calif.

Lenz, Clyde C., Ashton, Idaho.

Sexton, Bill, son Bobby, 231 E. Granite, Butte, Mont.

Hungerford, George; wife, from Hebgen Dam and West Yellowstone.

Sewain, C. H.; wife, Long Beach, Calif.

Hayward, Charles Jr., Ted, whole family all right.

Quisnell, Reed A.; wife, 3 children, Arcadia, Calif.

Keuning, A.; son, La Puenete, Calif.

Christensen, Roy, Rexburg, Idaho.

Guanne, Dennis E.; wife, 2 boys, Hunter, Utah.

People gone through the Ennis, Mont., Hospital:

Bennett, Mrs. P. R. and son, Phillip, 16, Coeur d'Alene, Idaho.

Lost, Mrs. Ruth, New York City.

Lost, Geraldin, New York City.

Lost, Shirley, New York City.

Frederick, Paul, Elyria, Ohio.

Delhart, Carol, Colville, Wash.

Lost, Joan, New York City.

Delhart, Danny, Colville, Wash.

Lost, Larry, New York City.

Mooge, Elsie, Spokane, Wash.

Smith, Ann, Greeley, Colo.

Smith, Jo Ann, Greeley, Colo.

Whittmore, George, Elyria, Ohio.

(End partial evacuee list)

Eugene B. and Mary Bair, care R. H. Hackson, route 2, Stone Mt., Ga.

Dave or Dale Covey, Billings.

Dean Dale, Billings.

Blue Evans (Forest Service reported him missing).

Edward T. and Elaine Egloff and children, Bruce,
Rick, Mike and Steve, Denver.
Melvin and Laura Frederick and children, Melva
and Paul J., Elyria, Ohio.
Thomas Goodman, Big Timber, Mont.
Johnnie Harr, Dillon, Mont.
Ray and Wilma Harrison and Bobbie, Linda and
Ray, no address.
Murlin Hartkoph and family, no address.
Laurel Haun, Billings.
Jerry Lavoi, Dillon.
Mrs. Elsie Moore, Spokane, Wash.
Rev. Elmer Ost and wife, Ruth (in Sheridan, Mont.,
hospital) and children, Joan, Geraldine, Shirley
and Larry, New York City.
Palmer Podd, Butte.
Martha Schrann, Butte.
Dick Slentz, Spokane.
Lewis and Ann Smith and daughters, Joan and
Carol, 1714 22nd Ave., Greeley, Colo.
Three children of Mr. and Mrs. E. H. Stryker,
San Mateo, Calif.
Gerald and Clara Taylor, no address.
Tom Travers, Denver.
Jack and Roseva Voucher and daughter, Joan Ann,
Oakview, Calif.
[Billings Gazette; August 21, 1959]

Some people refer to the 1959 Hebgen Lake Earthquake
as the Yellowstone Earthquake. Although the epicenter was
near the border of Yellowstone National Park, about 19 miles
from the northwestern side of the Yellowstone caldera, the
area most affected by the quake was in and around Hebgen
Lake and the Madison Canyon in Montana. This area is
where survivors were trapped because of a tremendous

mountain slide and a demolished roadway. Most of us spent a night and a day trapped at Refuge Point. Another small group of survivors by the landslide were rescued earlier in the day and taken to Ennis, Montana, by helicopter. Our family will always refer to it as the 1959 Hebgen Lake Earthquake.

The carefree days of walking along the Madison River. Cynthia in 1954 . Photo courtesy of Gloria Roberts

Chapter 9

Other Earthquake Damage

The Hebgen Lake Earthquake had a widespread affect. Some of the historic buildings at Mammoth Hot Springs in Yellowstone National Park were damaged. The famous Old Faithful Inn was evacuated. It had water damage caused by broken pipes. The chimney in the dining room crumbled and fell through the roof. There were several landslides in the Park that blocked roads. Streambeds were moved out of their original places. Hot springs had temperature changes and many of them appeared muddy. Around 200 geysers started to erupt at the same time, many of them new or dormant. According to the Park's assistant chief ranger at the time, Frank Sylvester, Old Faithful and other scenic features appeared to be undamaged. There were about 18,000 people staying in Yellowstone during the earthquake. Even though roads were badly cracked or covered in rocks, most people were able to find a way to drive out of the Park.

In West Yellowstone, Montana, chimneys were knocked over and window glass was shattered. Shops were damaged as well as the courthouse and the railroad station.

Telephone lines were down. Roads were severely beaten up.

Casualties were reported along Raynolds Pass on the Montana-Idaho border when a mountain slide supposedly hit the road. Later, it was determined that they were actually victims discovered near the Madison Landslide. Confusion and false reports were common after the quake.

Communities in Montana and Idaho also experienced the effects of the earthquake. There was damage to structures and a few minor injuries.

Meanwhile, back at the earthquake area, a multitude of problems needed solving. Roads had to be rebuilt or fixed. The dam required repairing as well as a channel dug to release water blocked by the slide. The water was rapidly rising at about nine feet per day in the newly formed Earthquake Lake. There was an overwhelming fear that the water would destroy Hebgen Dam or flow over the rockslide and flood towns downstream. The Army Corp of Engineers wasted no time digging a spillway across the blockage. It was finished in September of 1959. A great deal of erosion took place as the water flowed through the channel. To fix the problem, a new spillway was cut along the center a month later. This helped to lower Quake Lake by 50 feet.

Water was released from Hebgen Lake's reservoir in order to make repairs to the dam. There were several cracks in the core wall that needed grouting. The spillway at the dam was beyond repair and the entire structure was replaced.

Chapter 10

Facing Fear

We decided to face our fear the next summer and return to the scene of the disaster. We drove our yellow car, which gave us nothing but trouble after the quake. It was so messed up that it was continually in the shop being repaired for one thing or another. It began to match its color—a true lemon. We returned to the quake area with my dad's older sister and her family. Of course, we stayed in West Yellowstone this time. Our relatives desired to see the devastation from the earthquake and we wanted to see the mountain slide. It was not emotionally easy for us to drive back into Madison Canyon. Nancy had only been on one vacation and she was not sure she wanted to go on another one. We were all surprised that the roads were repaired so quickly and that we could drive into the canyon. A great deal was accomplished in a short period of time.

We were all totally in awe of what we observed. It was shocking to see the destruction of cabin homes, many of them immersed in the Quake Lake water. Pieces of the old crumbled road brought back terrifying memories of being trapped. The new lake appeared eerie with dead trees poking out of the water. A year earlier they provided shelter for birds, squirrels and shade for campers and picnickers. Halford Camp had vanished with its colorful totem pole, private picnic tables, bridges, winding dirt roads and quaint cabins. Everything floated away. It was sad to think that we were one of the last ones to stay in those cabins.

When we reached the landslide, we were amazed at how massive it was. At least half of the mountain had collapsed into the canyon below. Pictures in magazines did not do it justice.

The Madison Slide. Photo credit U.S. Geological Survey.

Several years later, my mother's sister and husband bought a cabin downstream from the slide and lived there year-round. At first I thought that they were crazy. It is still a bit creepy driving through the Madison Canyon. In spite of that, we still like to visit. We have even stayed between the dam and the slide at the Beaver Creek Campground. We have property in Island Park, Idaho, and my sister built a cabin there. We raised our children to love nature and we camped in Yellowstone National Park and the surrounding Greater Yellowstone Ecosystem. My mother states, "After a long time, you finally get over it."

The land in the Madison Canyon is healing, and our lives are healing, too.

**The Madison Slide one year later. Taken with the box camera.
Personal photo 1960.**

Chapter 11

Anniversaries

My mom, dad and sister went to most of the Hebgen Lake Quake commemorative anniversaries. My first anniversary was the 50th. Dad died a month before this anniversary. My brother, Jeff, who was born a few years after the quake, designed shirts for Mom, Nancy and me to wear. My husband, Doug, and my daughter Melinda and her husband, Lucas, came with us to the commemoration activities.

There were several events planned over the course of four days, which began on August 14, 2009. During the first two days, there were guest speakers at the Earthquake Lake Visitor Center. We hiked back to Refuge Point with Halford Camp historians Joanne Girvin, John Owen, and Dave Powers.

We also took a hike to see what was left of the ghost village, consisting of some of the old cabins from Halford Camp. When the cabins floated away after the quake, many of them landed in a meadow across the river. After fifty years, they were rapidly deteriorating. Most of the roofs were caved in at this point. One cabin ended up on our side of the river. We were able to look inside and take some pictures from the outside. My mother is almost certain that it was the cabin we stayed in. I could see a nail sticking out of the log that marked the place where Nancy's ball cap remained steadfast.

Deteriorated cabin from Halford Camp. Personal photo, 2009.

Looking inside the old cabin. Personal photo, 2009.

Remains of a structure. Personal photo, 2009.

On the morning of the next day, we returned to Refuge Point. We met and thanked some of the original smoke jumpers who were there to share their memories of August 18, 1959. After that, some current smoke jumpers staged a reenactment parachuting into Refuge Point. We all enjoyed the colorful parachutes dropping from the sky, just like they did 50 years before.

**Ghost Village in the distance, consisting of Halford Camp
Cabins. Personal photo, 2009**

**Original Forest Service Smoke Jumpers at the 50th anniversary.
Personal photo, 2009.**

In the afternoon, we met other survivors at the Holiday
Inn in West Yellowstone where stories and photographs
were shared and displayed. We visited with survivor Anita
Painter Thon. Her mother was one of the injured that died
in a hospital in Bozeman, Montana a few days after the

quake. Since the anniversary, Anita has written two books about the earthquake and its victims, *Shaken in the Night* and *The 28*. All of the stories from the survivors were exceptional. Of course, it would have been wonderful to hear each person's story. As my Dad wrote, "All had a story to tell."

Mildred (Tootie) Greene, one of the nurses that attended to the injured after the quake, helping a woman up the hill prior to the memorial service. Personal photo, 2009.

There were unsung heroes that I knew little about until this anniversary. One such account was about a man named George Hungerford who was the superintendent at the Hebgen Dam. His granddaughter spoke at the anniversary and gave us an account of his actions after the quake. Due to the weakened condition of the dam, George and his co-workers believed that it was critical to get as much water out of Hebgen Lake as possible. They devised a plan that turned out to be a complicated and tricky operation. They worked against the clock to clean and dry the generator in order to get it operational. Other technical tasks dealing with the stop logs were performed before water was released from the dam. This was all done during aftershocks and while gigantic boulders were flying off of the nearby cliffs. In the end, they were able to pump water from the dam before the generator blew. No doubt, George and his co-workers did their part to save our lives. George also provided a boat to aid in rescue operations. We were told the boat was used to save the couple clinging to life in the tree all night.

On one of the days while we were in the canyon enjoying anniversary events, two big black helicopters flew into the area. At that time, President Obama was there to visit Yellowstone National Park. We do not know if he decided to take a peek at the Madison River Canyon, or if it was the Secret Service.

At the Visitor Center with Joanne Girvin, Hebgen Quake expert from the Forest Service. Gloria, Cynthia and Nancy wearing our shirts made by our brother Jeff. Personal photo, 2009.

On the last day of the 50th anniversary, we climbed the trail to the massive dolomite boulder above the visitor center and attended a lovely memorial service on this sacred spot. We gazed at the plaque on the boulder bearing the names of the 28 earthquake casualties.

Memorial services at the 50th anniversary of the 1959 Hebgen Lake Earthquake. Personal Photo, 2009.

Survivors at the 50th anniversary outside the Holiday Inn in West Yellowstone, Montana. Personal Photo, 2009

Appendix A

Earthquake Terminology, Interesting Facts

In order to understand what was going on around us in this situation, earthquake terminology was a must, even for a child. Children today are much more aware of natural and man-made disasters. The world seems to be in constant turmoil. Back in the 1950's, we were more concerned about a nuclear attack. As a child, I participated in fire and nuclear attack drills but no earthquake drills. Earthquake drills are now common in schools and in our neighborhoods, which is important if you live in an area laced with faults. Many of the following terms were explained to me the day after the earthquake, while other interesting facts were discovered during the following year. These are basic definitions that made sense to me as a child.

Natural Disaster: A natural disaster is a catastrophic event such as an earthquake, hurricane, tsunami, tornado, flood, volcanic eruption or lightening-caused wildfire.

Earthquake: When an earthquake occurs, there is sudden

shaking and strong vibrations on the Earth's surface, or outer crust. It is caused by shock waves from fault movement or by a landslide. An earthquake can happen on land or at sea. Some are so small that they cannot be felt and others are violent and destructive, like the one we experienced the night of August 17, 1959. The power of the Hebgen Lake Earthquake was felt in eight states and in Canada. The cost of damage to roads, structures and timber was estimated to be around $11 million, which is about the same as $90 million today.

Tremor: An earth tremor is a term to describe an earthquake of low intensity. We called all of the aftershocks that we experienced at Refuge Point tremors, even though some were powerful.

Foreshock: A foreshock often occurs before the main earthquake. This initial burst of energy is often too small to be felt. The 1959 Hebgen Lake Earthquake had a foreshock immediately before the mainshock. It explains the initial scratching on the screen and the rattling of the doors that we first experienced.

Mainshock: The big event with all of the shaking, rocking and rolling is the mainshock. It can cause the surface of the earth to change drastically, as it did in the Madison River Canyon. The area experienced one of the largest amounts of displacement ever recorded.

Displacement: When something moves from its original position.

Aftershock: Shaking that happens at the location of the main shock after a powerful earthquake has occurred is an aftershock. They are frequent the day after the initial earthquake. They can continue for several days, weeks, months and even years. We experienced frequent and strong aftershocks while at Refuge Point.

Shock Waves, or Seismic Waves: Waves that are caused by the shifting of rock during an earthquake are shock waves, or seismic waves. Scientists measure their different travel times to locate the epicenter, or ground zero of a quake. These vibrations travel outward from the focus of the quake. The focus is the place inside the earth below the epicenter where the underground rock first begins to move.

Epicenter: The exact location on the surface of the earth where a fault ruptures is the epicenter. It is directly above the focus of the quake. The epicenter of the Hebgen Lake Earthquake was located at Duck Creek, which is at the junction of Highways 191 and 287 and eight miles north of West Yellowstone, Montana. It was highway 287 that was severely damaged and covered by the mountain slide.

Fault: A fault is a crack or fracture in the earth's crust, or outer layer. When pressure builds up, it causes shifting and slipping of the rocks along fault lines. This release of energy results in an earthquake. The crust of the earth can move up, down or to the side. The faults that were involved in the Hebgen Lake earthquake were the Red Canyon Fault, Hebgen Fault and Madison Range Fault. Blocks of earth and rock in between faults are called fault blocks. Each fault has an associated block. They are the Red Canyon Block, Hebgen Lake Block and the Missouri Flats Block. When the quake occurred, all three blocks sank immediately within seconds of each other. The Hebgen Lake and Red Canyon blocks tipped toward their northern boundaries. The Hebgen block caused the most destruction, which led to the northern end of the Hebgen Lake dropping 19 feet.

Scarp: A scarp occurs when one side of the ground is higher than the other due to the movement of the fault. There were large scarps left along fault lines in the area after the Hebgen Lake quake. Some of them stretched for miles and others were at least 20 feet high. The scarps are the result of dip-slip movement, or when fault blocks shift vertically. They can still be seen today, although some are covered with foliage.

A 19-foot Red Canyon fault scarp near Red Canyon Creek. Notice the man standing at the base of the fault scrap. Photo credit, U.S. Geological Survey.

Seiche marks on walls of a Hilgard Lodge unit. The marks show the height and number of the waves. Photo credit, U.S. Geological Survey.

Seiche: A seiche is a wave on the surface of a landlocked body of water. The French meaning of the word is "to sway back and forth." The water begins to sway due to seismic waves, windstorms, landslides, or by the tilting of the earth. The earthquake of August 17, 1959, caused seiches on Hebgen Lake as well as on bodies of water located in Montana, Wyoming, Idaho and Canada. Huge waves as high as 20 feet topped the Hebgen Lake Dam.

Fissure: Openings, or cracks in the ground, are called fissures. The Madison Canyon was covered with these after the quake.

Seismograph: An instrument that measures shock waves in the earth is a seismograph. The machine moves back and forth with the earth. A needle-like-pen is attached to a cylinder wrapped with paper to record the results. The picture drawn by the seismograph is a seismogram. According to my mother, the nearest seismograph at the time of the 1959 Hebgen Lake Earthquake was located at the University of Utah in Salt Lake City. The quake was so violent that it knocked the seismograph off scale for four minutes. Other seismograph machines suffered from the same fate. Scientists use readings from several different seismographs to determine the magnitude of a quake. There were too many inconsistencies with the machines that night. As a result, the actual duration and the magnitude of the quake proved difficult to determine. The duration of the earthquake is now reported to be about 40 seconds. My dad's wristwatch was ruined during the quake and stopped at 11:46 pm. Did it continue to tick for a while before it stopped? It ceased functioning before my dad grabbed it from the floor as we exited the cabin. My mother believes that the entire experience lasted for a long time. Perhaps it is because time seems to stand still during life threatening experiences.

Magnitude: The intensity or the strength of an earthquake is its magnitude. Because there was no way of knowing the exact magnitude of the 1959 Hebgen Lake Earthquake, scientists used whatever information they had available at the time. Over the years, the magnitude of the earthquake was reported to be anywhere from 6.9 to 7.9. Through research, scientists have now determined that the magnitude of the Hebgen Lake Quake was 7.5.

Richter Scale: The Richter scale indicates the amount of energy released by an earthquake, or its magnitude. The measurement was the invention of Charles F. Richter in 1935. The scale is logarithmic ranging from 1 to 10. A seismograph is used to gather information on the amplitude of the seismic waves to determine a number. Whole numbers on the scale increase by a factor of ten, which means that each increase of a whole number represents a 10-fold increase in magnitude. For example, a 7.0 earthquake is ten times stronger than a 6.0 earthquake, or 100 times stronger than a 5.0 earthquake. An earthquake with a magnitude of 5.0 or lower is minor while one that is 7.0 or larger is considered major. Today, scientists rely more on the moment magnitude scale, which measures the actual energy released by an earthquake and is considered more accurate.

Landslide: A landslide is a downward movement of debris, earth or rock from a slope. The Madison Canyon Landslide originated from a mountain with an unstable slope. The mountain was made up of weathered layers of rock consisting of schist and gneiss, as well as dolomite, a strong rock that maintained the slope. The dolomite was not able to hold after the mainshock hit. The Madison Canyon slide was one of the worst ones ever recorded in the history of the northwestern United States. About 50 million tons of earth, timber and rock swooped down the mountain traveling over 100 miles per hour. It took a matter of seconds for the slide to barrel down the mountain, cross the narrow canyon and plop down on the opposite side. As the slide traveled, air was trapped beneath it. When the air escaped, cyclone-like winds swept away trees, cars and, sadly, people. The slide also caused displacement of the Madison River. A wall of water uprooted trees and flooded tents and trailers. Today, the Earthquake Lake Visitor Center sits on the part of the slide that ended up on the opposite side of the canyon. In our case, the unbearable cracking sound was caused by the unstable rock breaking free from the mountain. The explosion occurred when the slide hit the canyon floor resulting in a force that knocked the cabin off of its foundation and a blast of wind that blew through the doors.

Madison Slide debris that traveled down the slope across the Madison River and up the north canyon wall. Photo credit U.S. Geological Survey.

Earthquake Lake, or Quake Lake: A new lake was formed when the landslide in the Madison Canyon blocked the flow of the Madison River. It is about 190 feet at its deepest part and 6 miles long. Scientists estimate that in 200 years, Quake

Lake will drain and the Madison River will return to its natural flow.

Rapidly growing Earthquake Lake blocked by the Madison Slide. Photo credit U.S. Geological Survey.

Appendix B

Earthquake Preparedness

Have a Flashlight

Many of us were awakened from a deep sleep in the dark of night when the 1959 Hebgen Lake Earthquake began. It takes a few seconds to realize what is happening. Being prepared makes it easier to cope with the unexpected. It is helpful to have a crank or battery-operated flashlight readily available. If using the battery-operated flashlight, have some extra batteries on hand. Our parents did have a flashlight the night of the earthquake. However, my dad forgot that he put the flashlight under his pillow and took off without it. That mistake caused a head injury when he slipped and fell in a room covered in water and debris. My mom remembered the flashlight and used it as we exited the cabin, which prevented the rest of us from having an accident.

Close Window Coverings

Close the drapes, blinds or shutters at night. If window

glass is broken, this prevents it from landing all over the floor. If you have to walk on it with bare feet, it is not easy. Believe me!

Secure Furniture and Water Heaters

Secure heavy items such as dressers, curio cabinets and water heaters. This prevents furniture from toppling over and reduces the possibility of objects hitting the floor. Securing a water heater can be done by a plumber or by an amateur. The water heater is secured by using metal straps attached to wall studs. Not only will this prevent a mess on the floor, it preserves water that may be needed later.

Store Heavy Items on Lower Shelves

Paper goods and non-breakable items are best stored on upper shelves and heavy items, bottles and jars on lower shelves. It is suggested to store food and water in different places in the home.

Keep a Change of Clothes Nearby

In the event of evacuation, have a change of clothes and shoes readily available. Of course, it is okay to wear pajamas. We all had to after the Hebgen Quake. Just make sure that they are not too embarrassing to be seen in public. Just ask my mom.

Have a Portable Radio for Emergencies

It is good to have a battery operated or a crank radio in case of any type of emergency. Listen to and follow public safety instructions.

Learn First Aid and Have a Kit

Be prepared with a first aid kit and learn the basic steps of providing first aid. Keep a kit in the home and one in the car.

Always Keep the Car Gas Tank at Least Half Full

Follow my dad's advice and always have a gas tank that is at least half full. This is critical if an evacuation becomes necessary. We were lucky because the Hebgen Lake area was not populated enough to cause a rush on gas stations by exiting people. Pumps may be damaged as well, making it impossible to get gas.

During A Quake

Stay calm. This advice is often easier said than done.

Think fast because if the earthquake is powerful, movement will be impossible as the shaking escalates.

Get down and try to crawl under a table or desk and hold on to the legs. If unable to get under something, protect your head and neck with your hands and arms.

Stay away from anything that might topple over such as cabinets, bookcases, and cupboards.

Stay away from windows.

If inside when the quake happens, stay there.

If outside when the quake hits, stay there. Do not approach buildings, trees, telephone or electrical lines.

When driving, stay away from overpasses and underpasses. Find a safe area to stop and stay in the vehicle.

If in a crowded store, do not run to the doorway. This will be the first place most people will try to go.

When in a tall building, get under a desk.

If in bed, stay there. Use a pillow as head protection. We did not think to use our pillows as head protection during the Hebgen Lake Earthquake. We had flying objects and mortar, or chinking, from the logs pelting us.

After A Quake

Always proceed with caution, no matter what.

Do not use elevators when in a building.

Be cautious around exits and stairways in case they are damaged.

Stay put unless there is a body of water close by. There might be a need to move inland or to get to higher ground. This is what we faced after the Hebgen Lake Quake.

If there is a smell of gas, open windows and shut off the main valve. Gas leaks cause explosions. Never light a match or any other kind of flame. Turn off pilot lights only if there is a gas leak. Otherwise, it might take days to get them back on again.

If electrical wiring seems damaged, shut off the power to avoid a fire or an electrical shock.

In the event that pipes are damaged, turn off the water where it enters the home.

Be aware that aftershocks will occur and more damage is possible.

Because it may take up to 72 hours before help arrives, store enough food and water for that period of time for each family member.

Give reassurance to others, especially children. Their biggest fear is losing their parents. Let them know that it is okay to be frightened and to talk about their fear.

Quote from my sister, Nancy Roberts: "I don't remember ever really being afraid or upset during the earthquake or the hours that followed. That was due to Mom and Dad not ever outwardly acting concerned or terrified of the dam breaking or a thousand other things that I am sure were going through their minds. Also, my sister never acted afraid or scared of what was happening. So, I credit all three with their composure under very scary and difficult circumstances."

Doug Brunnette and Nancy Roberts stand above a fault scarp.
Personal photo, 2009.

Mom sitting on Dad's fishing rock. The rock was once in the Madison River. Personal photo, 2009

About the Authors

Cynthia Roberts Brunnette is a graduate of Utah State University and lives in Kaysville, Utah. She is a freelance writer. Cynthia is married to Douglas Brunnette and is the mother of Amy Brunnette Green (Jeff), Brenden Brunnette (Emily), Maryanne Brunnette Martin (Michael) and Melinda Brunnette McGraw (Lucas). She is also the grandmother of 16 fantastic grandchildren.

Willard Dean Roberts was a World War II veteran. He graduated from the University of Utah and lived in Farmington Utah before his death. Dean is the husband of Gloria F. Roberts, father of Cynthia, Nancy, Jeffrey and grandfather of six.